W9-BAX-274

THE BRAIN IN YOUR BODY

BRIDGET HEOS

Britannica®
Educational Publishing

IN ASSOCIATION WITH

ROSEN
EDUCATIONAL SERVICES

Published in 2015 by Britannica Educational Publishing (a trademark of Encyclopædia Britannica, Inc.) in association with The Rosen Publishing Group, Inc.
29 East 21st Street, New York, NY 10010

Distributed exclusively by Rosen Publishing.
To see additional Britannica Educational Publishing titles, go to rosenpublishing.com

First Edition

Britannica Educational Publishing
J.E. Luebering: Director, Core Reference Group
Mary Rose McCudden: Editor, Britannica Student Encyclopedia

Rosen Publishing
Hope Lourie Killcoyne: Executive Editor
Jacob R. Steinberg: Editor
Nelson Sá: Art Director
Brian Garvey: Designer
Cindy Reiman: Photography Manager

Cataloging-in-Publication Data

Heos, Bridget, author.
The brain in your body/Bridget Heos. — First edition.
        pages cm. — (Let's find out! The human body)
Includes bibliographical references and index.
ISBN 978-1-62275-636-0 (library bound) — ISBN 978-1-62275-637-7 (pbk.) — ISBN 978-1-62275-638-4 (6-pack)
1. Brain — Juvenile literature. 2. Human body — Juvenile literature. 3. Human physiology — Juvenile literature. I. Title.
QP376.H33 2015
612.8'2 — dc23
                                                                                        2014020156

Manufactured in the United States of America.

Photo Credits: Cover, p. 1 © iStockphoto.com/RapidEye; interior pages background © iStockphoto.com/Firstsignal; pp. 4, 5, 8-9 (bottom), 10, 22, 25 Encyclopædia Britannica, Inc.; p. 6 moodboard/Thinkstock; p. 7 Blamb/Shutterstock.com; p. 9 (top) Anthony Correia/Shutterstock.com; p. 11 Dorling Kindersley/Thinkstock; p. 12 Original preparation by J. Klingler, Anatomical Museum, Basel, Switzerland; p. 13 Annaick Kermoal/Science Source; pp. 14, 16, 18 Roger Harris/Science Source; p. 15 BISP/Universal Images Group/Getty Images; p. 17 © Rubberball Productions/Getty Images; p. 19 Odua Images; p. 20 © Merriam-Webster Inc.; pp. 20-21 Professor P. M. Motta and D. Palermo/Science Source; p. 23 Mike Agliolo/Science Source; pp. 24-25 Purestock/Thinkstock; p. 26 ArtyVectors/iStock/Thinkstock; p. 27 Sergiy Zavgorodny/Shutterstock.com; p. 28 © AP Images; p. 29 © Photodisc/Thinkstock.

CONTENTS

WHAT IS THE BRAIN?

The brain is the organ that controls how all parts of your body work. It also controls your thoughts and feelings. The brain allows you to sense the outside world. The brain helps your body stay healthy and respond in the right way to its environment.

The brain is connected to the spinal cord. The spinal cord contains nerves that run to

brain

spinal cord

nerves

The nervous system allows the brain to communicate with the body. The nervous system is made up of the brain, the spinal cord, and nerves.

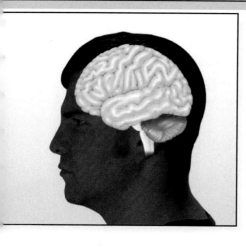

cerebrum

cerebellum

brain stem

◀◀

The human brain has three main parts: the cerebrum, the cerebellum, and the brain stem. Together they control how all parts of the human body work.

and from the brain. These nerves carry messages between the brain and the rest of the body. Together the brain, spinal cord, and nerves make up the nervous system.

The three main parts of the brain are called the cerebrum, the cerebellum, and the brain stem.

The **nervous system** processes information about the outside world as well as the inner workings of your body. The nerves send the information to the brain, which makes sense of the information. The brain then sends a message back through the nerves to tell the body how to react.

THE BRAIN STEM

The brain looks something like a mushroom. The "stem" of the mushroom is the brain stem. The brain stem is attached to the spinal cord. The brain stem controls the things that happen automatically in the body. This includes feeling hungry or thirsty or getting sleepy.

The lower part of the brain stem is called the medulla oblongata, or just medulla. The medulla controls important processes such as heartbeat and breathing. It also sends signals between the spinal cord and the upper parts of the brain.

Blood pressure tells us how strong the heart is beating. During a health checkup, the nurse checks a patient's blood pressure. Blood pressure is regulated by the medulla.

The medulla controls heartbeat, breathing, and other automatic processes. The pons is located above the medulla on the brain stem. It controls feeling in the face.

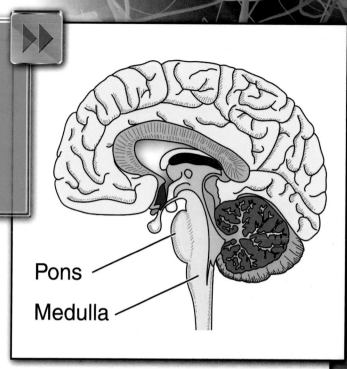

Pons

Medulla

THINK ABOUT IT

The brain stem controls automatic processes in the body such as hunger. Automatic processes are things that we cannot control. What are some other automatic processes that happen in our bodies?

Above the medulla is a part of the brain called the pons. The pons is associated with feeling in the face. The upper part of the brain stem is the midbrain. The midbrain helps with muscle control and eye movement. At the top of the brain stem are structures that control pleasure, pain, hunger, thirst, and body temperature. They also act as the relay center for all of the senses except smell and sight.

THE CEREBELLUM

The cerebellum is located just below and behind the brain stem and the cerebrum. It is much smaller than the cerebrum, but it has as many nerve cells as there are in all the other regions of the brain combined.

The cerebellum controls body movement. It is the part of the brain that allows people to learn motor skills. Unlike automatic processes, motor skills are movements that you decide to make. They include walking, skipping, and throwing a ball.

The cerebellum also helps people speak. Somebody with an injured cerebellum

> The cerebellum is located behind the brain stem. It allows people to learn new motor skills, such as running, skipping, and dancing.

Motor skills are physical movements that a person decides to make. How are motor skills different from automatic processes?

When a pitcher throws a ball he is using the part of the brain called the cerebellum. The cerebellum controls the movement of the muscles in his arms and legs to line up and throw a perfect pitch.

might have slow speech. He or she might also slur words.

pons

medulla oblongata

cerebellum

9

THE CEREBRUM

If the brain is something like a mushroom, the cerebrum is the "cap" of the mushroom. It accounts for two-thirds of the total weight of the brain. The cerebrum is the part of the brain that controls thinking. It also controls many other functions.

The cerebrum is divided into two **cerebral hemispheres**, or halves. The left hemisphere actually controls the right side

Lobes of the brain

parietal lobe

frontal lobe

occipital lobe

temporal lobe

The cerebrum controls thinking. It is made up of four lobes, or sections, that control different kinds of thought.

A **cerebral hemisphere** is either of the two halves of the cerebrum. The two halves are divided by a long fissure or separation.

of the body. The right hemisphere, in turn, controls the left side of the body.

The two halves work together, but sometimes one half has more control over certain activities than the other half. For example, for some people the left side seems to control language and speech while the right side controls emotions.

The two halves of the brain are separated by a deep groove. At the base of the groove is a bundle of nerves that allows the two halves to communicate and to work together.

Inside the Cerebral Hemispheres

Each hemisphere of the brain has an outer layer and an inner core. The outer layer is made up of material called gray matter. The inner core is made up of white matter. The gray matter is where thinking occurs. It is also where information is stored. The white matter helps with communication between different areas in the gray matter.

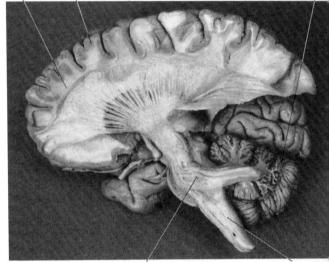

white matter   gray matter   cerebell[u]

pons   medulla oblong[a]

This photo shows one half of the brain—the left hemisphere. The darker outer layer is the gray matter, and the lighter inner core is the white matter.

The outer layer, or gray matter, is also called the cortex. The cerebral cortex has wrinkled ridges. These ridges are called gyri. They make the brain appear lumpy. "Sulci" is the name for the grooves between the gyri. The two most important sulci divide the brain into four sections, called lobes. These lobes are called the frontal, parietal, temporal, and occipital lobes.

THINK ABOUT IT

Sometimes in science, words have strange spellings or unusual forms. All the grooves in the brain together are called sulci (pronounced "sul-sigh"), but each individual groove is called a sulcus ("sul-kus"). All the ridges together are called gyri ("jai-rai"). What do you think we call each individual ridge?

The outer layer of the cerebrum has ridges called gyri. The grooves between the ridges are called sulci.

THE FRONT OF THE BRAIN

The frontal lobe is in the front part of the brain, behind the forehead. It is the largest of the four lobes. One of its jobs is to control a variety of movements. Damage to this area can result in weakness or paralysis on the opposite side of the body. Paralysis means that you cannot move your muscles.

The frontal lobe controls your conscience—the sense of what is right and what is wrong.

In 1848, a railroad worker named Phineas Gage had an accident, and a metal bar went through the frontal lobe of his brain. He survived, but the loss of parts of his frontal lobe changed his personality.

⏩

The frontal lobe also helps you understand the difference between right and wrong. It allows you to think about your actions and to make choices about how to behave. Knowing right from wrong and the feeling that you should do what is right is called your conscience.

THINK ABOUT IT

When was the last time you wanted to do something, but knew you might get in trouble if you did? That was your frontal lobe at work!

Where We Feel

The **parietal** ("puh-rie-i-tul") lobe is behind the frontal lobe. It contains the part of your brain that "feels" things. When you touch ice, scrape your knee, or pet a dog, the parietal lobe is where you feel these senses. Because of this lobe, you can detect the cold temperature of ice or the furry texture of a dog.

The parietal lobe is located behind the frontal lobe. When you touch something or hurt yourself, this part of the brain is activated.

The parietal lobe is also important in understanding language. Another one of its key tasks is awareness of your body and the space around it. A person with injuries to the parietal lobe may not understand the space around him or her well. For example, he or she may eat only the food on the right half of his or her plate.

Is this dog's fur soft or rough? Warm or cold? Wet or dry? The parietal lobe helps you understand this type of information.

Parietal is used to describe the parts of your body near the upper back wall of your head. It comes from a Latin word that means "of walls."

MEMORY AND VISION CENTERS

The temporal lobes are located on the sides of the brain. They help process sounds and memories. A sea horse-shaped area in the temporal lobe called the hippocampus is where short-term memories become long-term memories. Short-term memory is our ability to remember

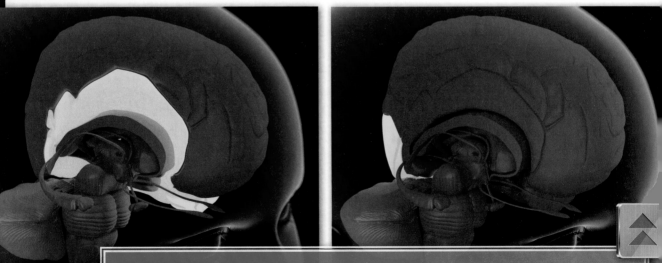

When a person remembers something that happened long ago, he or she is using the hippocampus. The hippocampus is located in the temporal lobe *(left)*. The occipital lobe *(right)* lies at the back of the brain.

THINK ABOUT IT

Alzheimer disease is an illness that attacks nerve cells in the brain. Patients with Alzheimer disease usually lose some of their memory. If Alzheimer disease affects your memory, which part of the brain do you think it attacks?

new information, such as the name of somebody we just met. Long-term memory is our ability to remember that information for a very long time, even years later!

The occipital ("ok-sip-it-ul") lobe is at the back of the brain. It is the visual center of the brain. The occipital lobe is where humans make sense of what they see. In the occipital lobe, signals from the eyes go through complex changes. After these changes, the brain can understand what the eyes are seeing.

The eye may be able to see things, but it's the brain that makes sense of what is seen, and that happens in the occipital lobe.

BRAIN CELLS

The human brain has two main types of cells: nerve cells, called neurons, and neuroglia. The neurons transport information. These cells are the basic working unit of the nervous system. Each neuron has parts that carry messages to and from the brain. These parts are

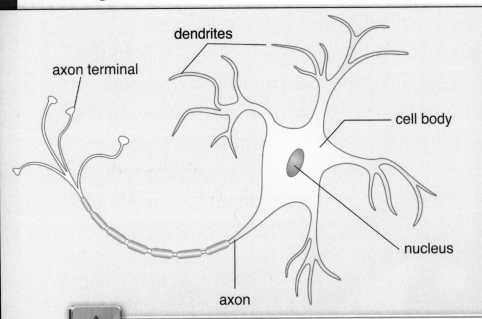

dendrites

axon terminal

cell body

nucleus

axon

Brain cells called neurons carry messages through the brain. Axons carry information away from the neuron to other cells. Dendrites accept information from the axons of other cells and carry it into the neuron.

THINK ABOUT IT

Scientists once thought that people were born with all the neurons they would ever have in life. Now they think people might produce some new neurons during their lifetime. Losing neurons causes memory loss and dementia. Why is it helpful for scientists to discover how we make new neurons?

called the axon and dendrites. The other type of cells are neuroglia. The neuroglia provide a protective environment for the neurons.

The brain contains about 100 billion neurons. We lose about 200,000 neurons each day! Because we have so many neurons, we don't notice the loss until we are very old. At that point, many people start to lose their memory or suffer from dementia. A person who has dementia cannot think clearly, understand, or remember.

We have many more neuroglia than neurons in our brains. The neuroglia provide an environment that helps neurons send and receive messages quickly.

THE INFORMATION FACTORY

The brain is like an information factory. Information is transferred along chains of interconnected neurons. Each neuron consists of a cell body with branches called dendrites and axons. Axons carry information away from the cell body. Dendrites carry information to the cell body.

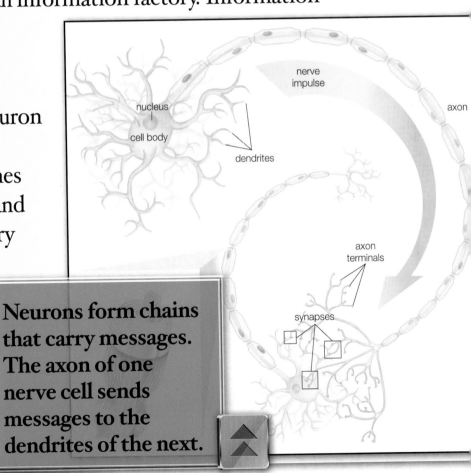

nerve impulse

nucleus

cell body

dendrites

axon

axon terminals

synapses

Neurons form chains that carry messages. The axon of one nerve cell sends messages to the dendrites of the next.

The gap between an axon and dendrite is called a synapse. Messages cross this synapse through an electrochemical process.

The transfer of information is an **electrochemical** process. An electrical impulse travels from the cell body through the axon. There is a small gap, called a synapse, between the axon of one neuron and the dendrite of the next neuron. At the end of the axon, there are tiny sacs that contain chemicals called neurotransmitters. When the electrical impulse reaches these sacs, they send neurotransmitters into the synapse. This sparks an electrical impulse in the next neuron.

Electrochemical processes change electrical energy into chemical energy, or the other way around.

THE BRAIN AND THE BODY

The spinal cord carries messages between the brain and the rest of the body. The spinal cord is made up of nerves. Nerves are cord-like collections of neurons. Nerves also branch out from the spinal cord and run throughout the whole body. There are two main types of nerves. Sensory nerves send information from the mouth, nose, skin, and other body parts to the spinal cord and brain. Motor nerves send information from the brain and spinal cord to the muscles and other body parts.

The spinal cord carries messages between the brain and body. The spinal cord is made up of nerves, and it is protected by the backbone.

When you step on something sharp, sensory nerves run to the brain and yell, "Ouch!" Motor nerves then tell you to lift your foot. In what ways are sensory nerves and motor nerves similar? What is one major difference in their jobs?

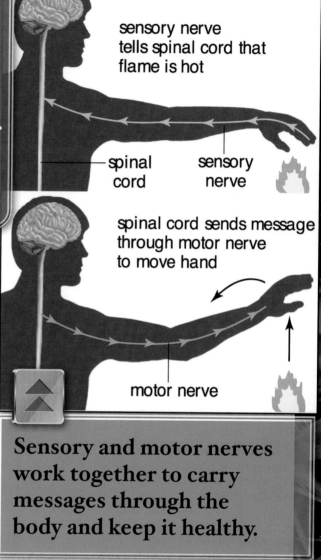

sensory nerve tells spinal cord that flame is hot

spinal cord

sensory nerve

spinal cord sends message through motor nerve to move hand

motor nerve

All of these nerves work together to protect the body and keep it working properly. For example, when a person touches a hot stove, the sensory nerves in the fingers send impulses to the spinal cord. The impulses say that the stove is too hot to touch. The spinal cord then sends impulses through motor nerves to the muscles of the arm. These impulses tell the muscles to pull the arm away from the stove.

Sensory and motor nerves work together to carry messages through the body and keep it healthy.

OUR NATURAL HELMET

The brain has a natural helmet that protects it. This helmet is made up of the skull and three membranes, or coverings, that surround the brain. The outer membrane is called the dura mater (which means "hard mother"). It is tough and fibrous. The middle membrane is called the arachnoid. The arachnoid is thin and weblike. The

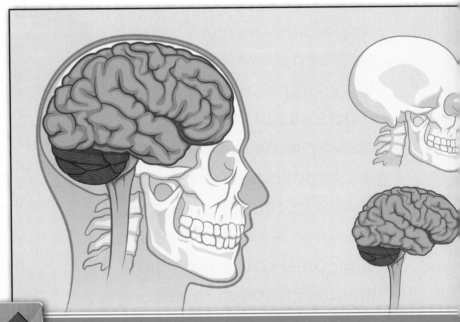

The skull and three membranes work together to form a helmet that protects the brain.

The brain is protected by a natural helmet. However, the skull cannot protect the brain from all injuries, so it is important to wear a helmet when skating, biking, or playing other sports.

inner covering is called the pia mater ("tender mother"). The pia mater is a delicate membrane that covers the surface of the brain.

Between the pia mater and arachnoid is a clear liquid. The brain floats in this liquid. This fluid is slippery and takes in shock. Like a helmet, it protects the brain from blows. It also brings nutrients to the brain. This fluid also surrounds the spinal cord.

COMPARE AND CONTRAST

The skull is a layer of bone that serves as an outer protection for the brain. Compare and contrast the skull and the liquid that surrounds the brain. How are they different?

Brain Injuries and Disorders

Even though it is protected, the brain can become injured. Hits to the head can cause serious injury. A brain can also be damaged if it does not receive enough blood because of a stroke or other condition. Depending on which part of the brain is injured, a person can have physical disabilities, problems with the senses, or changes in thought and behavior.

Brain injuries can happen while playing sports or during a car accident. After any hit to the head, it's important to see a doctor and make sure your brain is not injured.

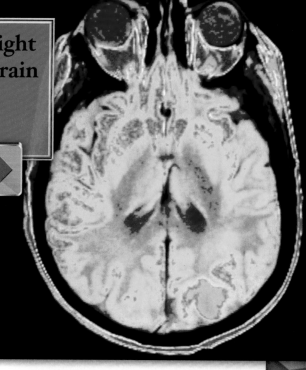

The bright blue area at the bottom right side of this image is a brain tumor. Brain tumors are caused by uncontrolled growth of brain cells.

The brain can also suffer from infections and diseases such as cancer. Other diseases, such as epilepsy, can be caused by problems with the electrical impulses in the brain.

Because of its key part in thinking and controlling the body, the brain is one of our most important organs. Thankfully, science keeps finding new ways to keep it healthy and to fix injuries. That's good news, because a healthy brain means a healthy body!

Epilepsy is a medical condition in the brain in which brain cells fire electrical signals too quickly. Too many signals cause seizures, or twitching muscles.

GLOSSARY

Alzheimer disease An illness that attacks nerve cells in the brain, causing loss of memory.

axon A strand of a neuron that carries nerve impulses away from the cell body.

brain stem The back and lower part of the brain including the midbrain, pons, and medulla oblongata.

cerebellum A large portion of the back part of the brain that controls body movement and speech.

cerebrum The part of the brain that controls thinking.

cortex The outer layer of gray matter on the cerebrum.

dendrite A strand of a neuron that carries nerve impulses toward the cell body.

lobe A rounded part of an organ in the body.

membrane A flexible sheet or layer, especially of a plant or animal part.

motor skill A learned movement of the muscles done on purpose.

nerve One of the stringy bands of tissue that connects the nervous system with other organs and carries nerve impulses.

nerve impulses Changes in electrical charges that move through the nervous system to carry messages between body parts and the brain.

nervous system The network of nerves and the brain in your body.

neuroglia Cells that protect neurons in the brain.

neuron A nerve cell; the basic working unit of the nervous system.

skull The case of bone that forms the skeleton of the head and surrounds the brain.

spinal cord The cord of nervous tissue that extends from the brain along the back.

For More Information

Books

Deak, JoAnn, and Sarah Ackerley. *Your Fantastic Elastic Brain*. San Francisco, CA: Little Pickle Press, 2010.

Halvorson, Karin. *Inside the Brain*. Minneapolis, MN: ABDO Publishing, 2013.

Schnurbush, Barbara. *Striped Shirts and Flowered Pants: A Story about Alzheimer's Disease for Young Children*. Washington, DC: Magination Press, 2007.

Stewart, Melissa. *How Is My Brain Like a Supercomputer? And Other Questions About the Human Body*. New York, NY: Sterling Children's Books, 2014.

Strange, Christopher M. *The Brain Explained*. New York, NY: Rosen Publishing, 2014.

Websites

Because of the changing nature of Internet links, Rosen Publishing has developed an online list of websites related to the subject of this book. This site is updated regularly. Please use this link to access this list:

http://www.rosenlinks.com/LFO/Brain

INDEX